Sunny-Side-Up Potato and Bacon Pizza, *page 98*

california pizza kitchen
taste of the seasons

Brian Sullivan with Paul Pszybylski
Photographs by Scott Goldsmith

fresh recipes that bring the CPK experience home

Published by CPK Management Company.
www.cpk.com

Library of Congress Cataloging-In-Data available upon request.

ISBN 978-0-986-38670-1 (pbk),
978-0-986-38671-8 (ebk)

Printed in United State of America.

10 9 8 7 6 5 4 3 2 1

acknowledgments

Every good cook knows that what they make can only be as good as the ingredients that go into it. Like the food our chefs create, this cookbook is the result of bringing together the finest ingredients.

First, this cookbook – and California Pizza Kitchen itself – would not have been possible without the hard work, skill, enthusiasm, and good humor of our team members. They have contributed, without measure, to the success of CPK over the last 30 years. In that time, we have grown from a single restaurant in Beverly Hills to more than 270 restaurants in over 208 cities around the world with the help of our business partners and suppliers. We dedicate this book to them.

CPK has always dared to be different, out front, and adventuresome. As we embark on our Next Chapter, we bring forward the best of our heritage, history, and soul with a fresh new look and new menu to provide an even more memorable dining experience.

We would like to express special appreciation to our chefs, Brian Sullivan and Paul Pszybylski, who bring culinary innovation to everything CPK, developing one-of-a-kind flavor combinations using fresh, local, seasonal ingredients combined in unexpected ways. In that spirit, Brian and Paul created unique recipes just for this book. They simply love food and want to share that passion.

Our overarching goal at California Pizza Kitchen is to make a genuine, human connection not only with every guest but with our employees and the communities in which we live and work. We continually strive to maintain our ROCK culture of Respect, Opportunity, Communication, and Kindness. Our Kindness Fund – a charitable fund established for and funded by CPK employees – helps fellow employees in need. Our Inspired Acts program is CPK's way of showing appreciation and support in our communities through projects that enhance their quality of life. Taking care of our people and our communities is part of our core philosophy.

Finally, we would like to express our gratitude to you and to all of our guests. We hope that you enjoy this cookbook. It features many new recipes – along with some of your favorites – to feed your curiosity and creativity as well as your friends and family!

Wild Mushroom Pizza, *page 75*

contents

introduction

Since the first California Pizza Kitchen opened in Beverly Hills in 1985, our passion has been to serve delicious, fresh, food in a warm, welcoming environment. As we celebrate our 30th year of doing just that, we launch into our Next Chapter, which features a new décor and a revitalized menu that reflects trends in food and the evolving tastes of our guests. And while much is changing, the three basic elements of the CPK experience haven't:

An inviting space. The first thing you see when step into a California Pizza Kitchen is a chef hand-tossing pizza dough in front of the flickering flames of a hearth oven. A bustling open kitchen is at the heart of a dining space created with reclaimed wood, steel, and a burst of green from the fresh herbs growing inside the restaurants. Vibrant artwork featuring local landmarks gives each restaurant its own distinct personality.

Fresh food. We cook what you want to eat – and the quality of our food starts with freshness. Our food is made from scratch at each of our restaurants. We take pride in introducing our guests to ingredients that may be new to them. We are now even more dedicated to highlighting locally sourced, peak-season produce. We care about where each ingredient comes from and how it was treated before and after it arrives in our kitchens. Our chefs travel all over the country tasting, learning, and finding inspiration they can bring to your meal.

Friendly faces. The CPK experience would not be the same without our people. Our employees bring a touch of "California creativity" to everything they do, as well as kindness, compassion, and a welcoming attitude.

Taste of the Seasons allows you to experience a bit of our CPK menu innovation in your home. We know that when you cook for family or friends, your wish is the same as ours – that the food you make adds to the happiness and comfort of the people you welcome to your table.

California Pizza Kitchen Executive Chairman and CEO G.J. Hart (center), the visionary of our Next Chapter transformation, shares a laugh in the CPK Innovation Kitchen with Paul Pszybylski (left), senior director of culinary innovation, and Brian Sullivan (right), senior vice president of culinary development.

spring

As the winter's chill gives way to the warmth of spring, nature seems to awaken. A new cycle of life begins, the landscape turns green and vibrant, and the palate is rewarded with light fresh offerings: peas, radishes, carrots, lettuces and greens – a refreshing change after the hearty foods of winter.

shaved vegetable salad

A mandoline slicer not only makes beautiful, paper-thin slices of vegetables, but it also makes very quick work of cutting vegetables in julienne. For this salad, shave the round vegetables – such as radish, cucumber, and fennel – in thin round coins. Shave the carrots lengthwise into long, thin ribbons, leaving about ½ inch of the green stem on for color.

Start to finish: 30 minutes   **Makes:** 2 main-dish or 4 side-dish servings

4	cups mixed field greens or mesclun
1	cup shaved watermelon radish*
1	cup shaved cucumber rounds (unpeeled)
1	cup shaved fennel**
1	cup snow peas, strings removed
1	cup shaved baby carrots (4 small or 2 large)
¼	cup chopped Italian parsley
5	tablespoons champagne vinaigrette (see recipe, page 46)
2	tablespoons capers cracked black pepper

1 Divide field greens among two large or four small chilled plates; set aside.

2 In a large bowl combine radish, cucumber, fennel, snow peas, carrots, and parsley. Drizzle with champagne vinaigrette, and toss gently to combine and coat.

3 Divide vegetables among plates, then place in a mound on top of greens. Garnish each salad with capers and cracked black pepper.

*tip Watermelon radish is an heirloom Chinese daikon radish. It is much larger than a standard garden radish and has a mild, slightly peppery flavor with some sweetness. Its flesh is white closest to the exterior and becomes pink and magenta toward the center – which accounts for its name. Cut large radishes in half before slicing.

**tip Cut large fennel bulbs in half before slicing.

hot-smoked salmon with tarragon remoulade

It's amazing how much smoke flavor the salmon absorbs in just 25 minutes. Most stove-top smokers come with very finely textured wood chips, but you can use regular chips as well. In general, fruit-bearing woods such as apple and cherry impart a more delicate flavor than nut-bearing woods such as oak and hickory.

Prep: 20 minutes   **Cook:** 25 minutes   **Makes:** 4 to 6 servings

remoulade

- ½   cup mayonnaise
- 1   tablespoon Dijon mustard
- 1   tablespoon finely chopped chives
- 1   tablespoon minced fresh parsley
- 1½   teaspoons minced fresh tarragon
- 1½   teaspoons Crystal Hot Sauce or ¾ teaspoon Tabasco*
- ½   teaspoon fresh lemon juice
- ¼   teaspoon cracked black pepper

salmon

- applewood chips (or your favorite wood chips)
- 1   12-ounce salmon filet
- 1   teaspoon fresh lemon juice
- ¼   teaspoon smoked paprika
- ¼   teaspoon kosher salt
- olive oil

to serve

- lightly toasted bread

1 For the remoulade, in a medium bowl combine mayonnaise, mustard, chives, parsley, tarragon, hot sauce, lemon juice, and cracked black pepper. Stir to combine. Cover and refrigerate until ready to use.

2 For the salmon, set up a stove-top smoker according to manufacturer's directions, using applewood chips.

3 Brush fish with lemon juice and season with smoked paprika and salt. Brush smoker rack lightly with olive oil. Place salmon on the rack. (If you are using a skin-on filet, place it on the rack skin side down.) Smoke over medium heat for 25 minutes or until salmon reaches 120°F.

4 Remove salmon from smoker. Let rest for 5 minutes before serving with remoulade and toasted bread.

*tip Crystal Hot Sauce is a medium-heat Louisiana hot sauce that is milder than Tabasco. If you use Tabasco, cut the amount of hot sauce in half.

A coho salmon swims through ocean kelp in waters near Seattle. Coho salmon are known for their unique taste, a true delicacy in spring.

bianco flatbreads

This decadently indulgent and delicious flatbread is slathered with truffle cream and topped with three cheeses – Gorgonzola, mozzarella, and mild and meltable queso quesadilla. Its richness makes it a terrific appetizer for sharing.

Prep: 20 minutes   **Bake:** 6 minutes per flatbread   **Makes:** 4 (12×4-inch) flatbreads

	all-purpose flour
2	portions hand-tossed pizza dough, at room temperature (see recipe, page 24)
1	cup heavy whipping cream
1	teaspoon truffle-infused olive oil
¼	cup crumbled Gorgonzola cheese
1	cup shredded mozzarella cheese
¼	cup shredded queso quesadilla cheese
2	ounces fresh mozzarella cheese, torn into ½-inch pieces
16	large fresh sage leaves
4	teaspoons grated Parmesan cheese

1 Heat oven to 500°F. If using a baking stone, arrange a rack in the upper third of the oven and place stone on rack. Heat for 1 hour. (If using a baking sheet, arrange rack in middle of oven.)

2 On a lightly floured surface, cut one portion of dough in half. Working with one half at a time, shape into a rough oval. Using a rolling pin, roll dough into a long, narrow oval, approximately 12×4 inches. Lightly sprinkle a pizza peel or rimless baking sheet with flour. Transfer dough oval to prepared peel.

3 With an electric mixer whip cream and truffle-infused olive oil to stiff peaks. Spread three tablespoon-size dollops of truffle cream over dough oval. Top with one-fourth of the Gorgonzola, one-fourth of the shredded mozzarella, and one-fourth of the queso quesadilla. Evenly distribute one-fourth of the fresh mozzarella over the flatbreads. Place four sage leaves on each flatbread, making sure the leaves are upside down over a piece of fresh mozzarella.

4 Using small, quick back-and-forth movements, slide flatbread from peel onto hot pizza stone. (If using a baking sheet, place sheet on rack in oven.)

5 Bake until crust is lightly charred, about 6 to 8 minutes, popping bubbles with a spoon as needed.

6 Cut flatbread on the bias into four slices. Sprinkle with 1 teaspoon of the Parmesan. Serve immediately. Repeat with remaining dough and toppings.

Perfectly stretched hand-tossed pizza dough is thin and flat in the center but even in thickness with a rim that retains air from the proofing process so that the heat from the oven creates a crisp, airy crust.

hand-tossed pizza dough

Prep: 20 minutes   **Stand:** 2 hours   **Makes:** 4 (11-inch) pizza crusts

- 4¾ cups all-purpose flour, plus more for shaping dough
- 2½ teaspoons fine sea salt
- 1 teaspoon sugar
- 2½ teaspoons active dry yeast
- 2½ teaspoons extra virgin olive oil
- 2 cups lukewarm water

1 In the bowl of a stand mixer fitted with a dough hook, whisk the 4¾ cups flour, salt, sugar, and yeast. Add oil and the water, beating on low speed until dough is smooth. Divide into four balls. Place each in a separate bowl covered with plastic wrap. Let rise at room temperature (about 70°F) in a draft-free area until dough has more than doubled in size, about 2 to 2½ hours. Shape according to directions in recipe.

2 Use immediately or follow directions for storage.

short-term storage Can be made up to 3 days ahead. Place each dough ball in a separate bowl covered with plastic wrap; chill. To use, let bowls sit at room temperature covered with plastic wrap for 2 to 3 hours, or until dough has more than doubled in size.

long-term storage Can be made up to 3 months ahead. Immediately after shaping, wrap each dough ball separately in plastic wrap. Place dough balls in a large freezer bag. Seal, label, and freeze. To use, unwrap desired number of dough balls and place each in its own bowl covered with plastic wrap. Thaw in the refrigerator overnight. Let bowls sit at room temperature covered in plastic wrap for 2 to 3 hours or until dough has more than doubled in size.

roasted garlic chicken pizza

Mild, sweet spring onions are different than the mature scallions that are in season in spring. Thinly sliced lengthwise, they add flavor and eye-catching visual appeal to this pizza.

Prep: 30 minutes   **Roast:** 5 minutes   **Bake:** 6 minutes per pizza   **Makes:** 2 (11-inch) pizzas

all-purpose flour

2 portions hand-tossed pizza dough, at room temperature (see recipe, page 24)

2 spring onions, thinly sliced lengthwise

kosher salt

freshly ground black pepper

2 tablespoons extra virgin olive oil, plus additional for roasting onions

1 cup shredded mozzarella cheese

3 ounces fresh mozzarella cheese, cut into ¼-inch-thick slices

caramelized onions (see recipe, page 118)

6 ounces grilled chicken breast, pulled into ¼-inch-thick slices

2 tablespoons grated Parmesan cheese

roasted garlic (see recipe, page 118)

1 teaspoon cracked black pepper

1 Preheat oven to 500°F. If using a baking stone, arrange a rack in the upper third of the oven and place stone on rack. Heat for 1 hour. (If using a baking sheet, arrange rack in middle of oven.)

2 Lightly flour a work surface. Place one portion of dough on the surface, being careful to maintain the round shape and thickness of the dough; do not press. Lightly flour the top of the dough. Using your index fingers, press a 1-inch rim around the outer edge of the circle. Once rim is formed, press air out of the center of the dough, being careful not to flatten the rim. Using your knuckles, from the bottom of the dough, carefully stretch the dough, rotating as you work, to form an 11-inch circle. Take care to maintain a uniform thickness in the center. Gently toss dough in the air a few times. Set aside and repeat with remaining ball of dough. Lightly sprinkle a pizza peel or rimless baking sheet with flour. Transfer one dough circle to prepared peel. (See pages 24–25.) (If using a baking sheet, lightly flour the baking sheet. Transfer one dough circle to prepared sheet.)

3 Arrange spring onion slices on a baking sheet. Drizzle with a little olive oil. Season with salt and pepper. Roast until just starting to brown, about 5 minutes; cool.

4 Brush 1 tablespoon of the olive oil over the dough. Distribute ½ cup of the shredded mozzarella and half of the fresh mozzarella over the dough. Top with half of the caramelized onions, half of the grilled chicken, 1 tablespoon of the Parmesan, and half of the spring onions. Squeeze roasted garlic cloves from skins. Roughly chop. Distribute half of the chopped roasted garlic and ½ teaspoon of the cracked black pepper over the dough.

5 Using small, quick back-and-forth movements, slide pizza from peel onto hot stone. (If using a baking sheet, place sheet on rack in oven.)

6 Bake, rotating pizza halfway through baking time, until bottom of crust is crisp and top is blistered, 6 to 8 minutes. Repeat with remaining dough circle and toppings.

gnudi with spring peas

Gnudi ("nyOO-dee") are very similar to gnocchi. The main difference between these two types of dumplings is that gnudi contain ricotta in place of the potatoes that are the base of gnocchi. These light, airy dumplings are tossed in a cream sauce flavored with Italian bacon and brightened by the sweetness of two kinds of peas.

Prep: 40 minutes   **Stand:** 30 minutes   **Chill:** 2 hours   **Cook:** 18 minutes   **Makes:** 6 servings

gnudi

1   15-ounce container whole-milk ricotta cheese
½   cup grated Parmigiano-Reggiano cheese
¼   cup grated Romano cheese
¾   cup all-purpose flour, plus more for dusting
1   large egg plus 1 egg yolk, lightly beaten
½   teaspoon kosher salt
½   teaspoon cracked black pepper

to serve

4   ounces pancetta, roughly chopped
1½   cups sugar snap peas, cut in half lengthwise
1   cup English peas, fresh or frozen
2½   cups heavy whipping cream
¼   cup grated Parmigiano-Reggiano cheese
    cracked black pepper

1   Line a medium bowl with several layers of paper towels. Place ricotta cheese in bowl and allow to drain for 30 minutes.

2   In a large bowl combine drained ricotta, Parmigiano-Reggiano, Romano, ¾ cup flour, egg and egg yolk, salt, and pepper. Stir gently until well combined. Mixture should be moist and have some small pieces of ricotta remaining. (Add extra flour, 1 tablespoon at a time, if mixture feels too wet.)

3   Dust a large rimmed baking sheet generously with flour (a shaker or flour sifter works best for this). Using two teaspoons, shape ½-tablespoon portions of dough into 48 football shapes. Place on floured baking sheet. Dust gnudi with more flour. Cover loosely with plastic wrap and refrigerate for 2 hours.

4   When ready to serve, bring a large pot of salted water to a gentle boil. Carefully add half of the gnudi to the pot. Cook for 3 minutes or until cooked through and tender. Use a slotted spoon to remove from pot. Drain in a colander while cooking the other half of the gnudi.

5   Meanwhile, in a large sauté pan cook pancetta over medium heat until browned and cooked through, about 7 minutes. Drain off as much fat as you can. Add snap peas and English peas, and stir gently to combine. Add cream and bring to a gentle boil across the entire surface of the cream. Simmer and reduce for about 5 minutes.

6   When gnudi are cooked and drained, add to cream sauce. Stir gently to coat them.

7   To serve, spoon some of the peas and pancetta in cream sauce in each of six warmed pasta bowls. Carefully spoon eight gnudi and some of the remaining cream sauce and peas on top of peas and pancetta in bowls. Top each serving with grated Parmigiano-Reggiano and cracked black pepper. Serve immediately.

chicken milanese

Checca ("KEE-ka") is an uncooked tomato sauce made with ripe Roma tomatoes, basil, olive oil, and garlic. Together with peppery arugula and a squeeze of lemon, it gives a fresh touch to this classic Italian dish of crispy breaded and pan-fried chicken cutlets.

Prep: 50 minutes   **Cook:** 5 minutes per batch   **Makes:** 4 servings

checca

4	medium Roma tomatoes, seeded and diced
1	garlic clove, minced
1	tablespoon chopped fresh basil
2	tablespoons extra virgin olive oil
½	teaspoon kosher salt

chicken

2	cups panko bread crumbs
1½	teaspoons kosher salt
1½	teaspoons dried basil
1	teaspoon ground white pepper
2	large eggs, beaten
4	8-ounce boneless, skinless chicken breast halves, split in half horizontally (to create 8 thin pieces total)
¼	cup olive oil, plus additional if needed

to serve

8	cups loosely packed baby arugula
½	cup shaved Parmesan cheese
2	small lemons, halved

1 Preheat oven to 225°F. For the checca, in a small bowl combine tomatoes, garlic, fresh basil, olive oil, and salt. Stir to combine; set aside.

2 For the chicken, in a shallow dish combine bread crumbs, salt, dried basil, and white pepper. Stir to thoroughly mix; set aside. Place beaten eggs in another shallow dish; set aside.

3 Place each piece of chicken between two pieces of plastic wrap. Using the flat side of a meat mallet, pound chicken lightly to about ¼ inch thick. Working with one piece at a time, dip chicken in eggs, turning to coat both sides. Gently shake off excess. Coat chicken on both sides with seasoned bread crumbs; set aside. Repeat with remaining seven pieces of chicken.

4 In an extra-large sauté pan heat ¼ cup olive oil over medium heat. Cook chicken in batches for 5 to 7 minutes, turning once, until chicken is no longer pink. Transfer cooked chicken to a paper towel-lined baking sheet and keep warm in the oven while cooking remaining chicken. If needed, add additional oil to pan through the cooking process. Turn heat down if oil starts to smoke.

5 To serve, place two pieces of chicken side by side at a slight angle in the center of a large plate. Top with a row of arugula, leaving the sides of the chicken slightly uncovered. Drain off and reserve excess liquid from the checca. Drizzle the liquid over the arugula; spoon drained checca over the arugula. Neatly arrange shaved Parmesan on top of checca and arugula. Add a lemon half to each plate and serve immediately.

salted caramel pudding

A sprinkle of salt enhances the buttery flavor of the caramel sauce in this layered parfait-style dessert. Look for flaked sea salt – the most widely available type is Maldon from England – to truly heighten the contrast between the creamy topping and the crunchy salt.

Prep: 45 minutes   **Cook:** 25 minutes   **Cool:** 30 minutes   **Chill:** 4 hours   **Makes:** 8 to 10 servings

caramel sauce

1   cup light corn syrup
1   cup granulated sugar
1   cup heavy whipping cream

pudding

2¼   cups whole milk
6   tablespoons cornstarch
10   large egg yolks, lightly beaten
2¼   cups heavy whipping cream
⅓   cup packed light brown sugar
¼   teaspoon kosher salt
1   teaspoon vanilla extract

to serve

8   to 10 purchased chocolate cookie wafers
1   cup sweetened whipped cream (see recipe, below) flaked sea salt

1   For the caramel sauce, heat corn syrup in a heavy-bottom 3- to 4-quart saucepan over medium-low heat, stirring occasionally, until it reaches 210°F, about 4 to 5 minutes.

2   Add granulated sugar and stir to combine. Continue cooking, stirring occasionally, until mixture is 320°F, about 10 to 12 minutes. Remove pan from heat and add cream. (Stand back for a moment, as mixture may foam up and spatter.) Whisk carefully until well combined. Allow caramel sauce to cool to 100°F to 110°F, about 30 to 40 minutes.

3   Meanwhile, for the pudding, in a heavy-bottom 3- to 4-quart saucepan whisk together milk and cornstarch. Add egg yolks, cream, brown sugar, and salt, and whisk until all ingredients are well combined.

4   Cook milk mixture over medium heat, stirring constantly, until mixture has reached 140°F, about 5 minutes. Add 1¾ cups of the warm caramel sauce (100°F to 110°F) and whisk until well combined. (Remaining caramel sauce will be used when assembling puddings. Store in the refrigerator until ready to serve.)

5   Continue to cook mixture until it reaches about 180°F and is thickened, whisking constantly, about 4 to 5 minutes. Once mixture reaches 180°F, it will thicken quickly, so watch carefully. Strain mixture through a fine-mesh strainer into a chilled bowl. Stir in vanilla. Place plastic wrap directly on surface to keep a skin from forming on top of the pudding. Chill at least 4 hours or overnight.

6   To serve, crumble one chocolate cookie wafer in the bottom of a 4-inch Mason jar or small bowl, then add ½ cup of the pudding. Top with 1 tablespoon of the sweetened whipped cream. Warm reserved caramel sauce in 10-second increments in the microwave to desired consistency. Drizzle whipped cream with caramel sauce. Top with flaked sea salt. Serve immediately.

sweetened whipped cream   To make 1 cup sweetened whipped cream, combine ½ cup heavy whipping cream, 1 to 2 teaspoons granulated sugar, and ¼ teaspoon vanilla extract in a chilled medium bowl. Whisk or beat with an electric mixer on low speed until soft peaks form.

Boats belonging to Lummi Island Wild Reefnet Salmon Fishery float in the waters of Bellingham Bay near Bellingham, Washington. CPK chefs visited the fishery – the only solar-powered fishery in the world – to learn

about its sustainable practices, which include using an ancient fishing method that captures the fish without creating air, water, or noise disturbances.

ginger tangerine cooler

This bubbly and refreshing nonalcoholic drink calls for orange-tangerine flavor syrup. If you can't find it, you can use a plain orange syrup instead.

Start to finish: 5 minutes   **Makes:** 1 drink

2	orange wedges
2	thin ginger coins*
	ice
¾	ounce orange-tangerine syrup (for coffee and cocktails)
¼	cup lemonade
¼	cup citrus soda (such as Fresca®), chilled
¼	cup club soda, chilled
	thin orange wedge, for garnish

Squeeze the two orange wedges into a cocktail shaker; drop wedges into shaker. Add ginger slices to shaker and fill with ice. Add syrup and lemonade. Cover and shake vigorously for 20 seconds. Pour into a 16-ounce glass (do not strain). Add more ice to glass. Top with citrus soda and club soda. Pour drink from glass back into cocktail shaker and back into glass to blend ingredients. Garnish edge of glass with thin orange wedge and serve immediately.

*tip The ginger does not need to be peeled; just slice it into ¼-inch-thick "coins."

coconut blossom

Be sure to use cream of coconut – not coconut milk – in this tropically inspired cocktail. Cream of coconut is thicker and sweeter than coconut milk. Look for it in the liquor aisle of your supermarket or at a liquor store.

Start to finish: 5 minutes   **Makes:** 1 drink

1	¼-inch-thick slice fresh pineapple, cut into 8 pieces
	ice
1	ounce mandarin-flavor vodka
1	ounce tequila blanco
2	ounces fresh agave sour (see recipe, page 114)
1	ounce cream of coconut
	pineapple leaf, for garnish

Place pineapple pieces in a cocktail shaker. Fill shaker with ice. Add vodka, tequila, fresh agave sour, and cream of coconut. Cover and shake vigorously for 15 seconds. Pour into a Tom Collins glass (do not strain). Add more ice, if necessary. Garnish with a pineapple leaf and serve immediately.

summer

The pleasures that summer brings are almost beyond measure. Farmer's Markets burst with so many varieties of produce at their peak – tomatoes, corn, melon, cucumbers, and peppers, along with perfectly ripened strawberries and peaches – all exploding with flavor and color. What better way to spend a summer evening than enjoying them al fresco along with a delicious steak cooked on the grill?

miso mango salad

The unique taste of miso – salty yet slightly sweet – is enhanced with honey and nutty sesame oil in the dressing for this colorful salad that combines mango, tomatoes, baby kale, crunchy jicama, and cucumbers with homemade pickled peppers. The pickled peppers need to sit in the vinegar mixture for a minimum of 12 hours, so it's best to make them a day ahead.

Prep: 40 minutes   **Chill:** 12 hours   **Makes:** 2 main-dish or 4 side-dish servings

- 2   cups diced ripe mango
- 2   cups baby kale
- 1½   cups Campari tomatoes, halved
- 1   small cucumber, cut into ¾-inch cubes
- 1   cup diced jicama, cut into ½-inch cubes
- 1   cup drained pickled peppers (see recipe, right)
- 1   tablespoon chopped fresh cilantro
- 1   tablespoon chopped fresh mint
- ⅓   cup honey miso dressing (see recipe, below)
- 1   teaspoon black sesame seeds, toasted

1 In a large bowl combine mango, kale, tomatoes, cucumber, jicama, pickled peppers, cilantro, mint, and honey miso dressing. Toss gently to coat.

2 Divide salad among two large or four small chilled plates.

3 Sprinkle each salad with sesame seeds; serve immediately.

pickled peppers In medium nonreactive bowl (glass or stainless steel) combine 1 cup red wine vinegar, ½ cup apple cider vinegar, ½ cup water, ½ cup granulated sugar, and 1 teaspoon salt. Whisk until salt and sugar dissolve completely. Add one-fourth of a medium red onion, thinly sliced; one-half of a medium red bell pepper, thinly sliced; and one-half of a medium yellow bell pepper, thinly sliced. Toss to combine, making sure vegetables are covered in liquid. Cover tightly with plastic wrap and chill for 12 to 24 hours before using. Store the drained vegetables you don't use for the salad in a tightly sealed container in the refrigerator for up to 3 days; use for salads, sandwiches, and wraps.

honey miso dressing In a blender combine ½ cup white miso, ⅓ cup honey, ¼ cup champagne vinegar, ¼ cup sesame oil, and ¼ teaspoon cracked black pepper. Blend on high until completely smooth. Makes 1 cup. Store in a tightly sealed container in the refrigerator for up to 2 weeks.

california field salad

Pretty in shades of pink and green, this mixture of lettuces, watermelon, and strawberries dressed in champagne vinaigrette pairs beautifully with grilled or roasted chicken or salmon.

Start to finish: 30 minutes   **Makes:** 2 main-dish or 4 side-dish servings

5   cups mixed field greens or mesclun

3   cups cubed watermelon

1½ cups thinly sliced strawberries

¼   cup chiffonade-cut fresh basil (see tip, page 116)

¼   cup champagne vinaigrette (see recipe, right)

¼   cup crumbled feta cheese

¼   cup roughly chopped pistachios

1 In a large bowl combine greens, watermelon, strawberries, basil, and champagne vinaigrette. Toss gently to evenly coat.

2 Divide among two large or four small chilled plates, making sure all ingredients are evenly distributed throughout each serving. Sprinkle with feta and pistachios. Serve immediately.

champagne vinaigrette In a blender container combine ½ cup champagne vinegar; 2 tablespoons honey; 1 tablespoon Dijon mustard; 1 teaspoon finely grated lemon peel; 1 tablespoon freshly squeezed lemon juice; 1 teaspoon finely chopped shallot; ½ clove garlic, coarsely chopped; ½ teaspoon kosher salt; and ½ teaspoon cracked black pepper. With the blender running on high, slowly add ¾ cup extra virgin olive oil in a thin stream until vinaigrette is slightly thickened and smooth. Store in a tightly sealed container in the refrigerator for up to 3 days. Makes 1¼ cups.

bbq chicken pizza

Although we would be hard-pressed to pick our favorite pizza, this iconic classic – an invention of CPK – has remained a best seller at our restaurants across the country for years. There are now many versions of barbecue chicken pizza out there, but we think the combination of sweet and saucy grilled chicken and smoked Gouda on an airy, delightfully chewy hand-tossed crust keeps our guests coming back again and again.

Prep: 30 minutes   **Bake:** 6 minutes per pizza   **Makes:** 2 (11-inch) pizzas

½ cup plus 2 tablespoons of your favorite barbecue sauce

6 ounces grilled chicken breast, pulled into ¼-inch-thick slices

all-purpose flour

2 portions hand-tossed pizza dough, at room temperature (see recipe, page 24)

1 cup shredded smoked Gouda cheese

1½ cups shredded mozzarella cheese

½ of a small red onion, sliced into ⅛-inch-thick rings

2 tablespoons chopped fresh cilantro

1 Preheat oven to 500°F. If using a baking stone, arrange a rack in the upper third of the oven and place stone on rack. Heat for 1 hour. (If using a baking sheet, arrange rack in middle of oven.)

2 In a small bowl combine ¼ cup of the barbecue sauce and the chicken. Toss well to combine; set aside.

3 Lightly flour a work surface. Place one portion of dough on the surface, being careful to maintain the round shape and thickness of the dough; do not press. Lightly flour the top of the dough. Using your index fingers, press a 1-inch rim around the outer edge of the circle. Once rim is formed, press air out of the center of the dough, being careful not to flatten the rim. Using your knuckles, from the bottom of the dough, carefully stretch the dough, rotating as you work, to form an 11-inch circle. Take care to maintain a uniform thickness in the center. Gently toss dough in the air a few times. Set aside and repeat with remaining ball of dough. Lightly sprinkle a pizza peel or rimless baking sheet with flour. Transfer one dough circle to prepared peel. (If using a baking sheet, lightly flour the baking sheet. Transfer one dough circle to prepared sheet.)

4 Top dough circle on peel with 2 tablespoons barbecue sauce, spreading evenly to base of rim. Top with ½ cup smoked Gouda and ¾ cup mozzarella. Top with half of the onion and half of the chicken.

5 Using small, quick back-and-forth movements, slide pizza from peel onto hot pizza stone. (If using a baking sheet, place sheet on rack in oven.) Bake, rotating pizza halfway through baking time, until bottom of crust is crisp and top is blistered, 6 to 8 minutes.

6 Drizzle about 1 tablespoon of the remaining barbecue sauce over the cooked pizza. Top with 1 tablespoon of the chopped cilantro; serve immediately. Repeat with remaining dough circle and toppings.

burrata margherita pizza

Burrata is a small, pouch-shape cheese that is a variation on fresh mozzarella, but with thickened cream inside. It has a very delicate flavor and texture. On this most classic Neapolitan pizza, the Burrata is placed on the hot crust just long enough for the cheese to warm and spread slightly before serving. Buy Burrata no more than a few days before before you plan to use it, as it is a fresh cheese and does not have a long shelf life.

Prep: 20 minutes   **Bake:** 5 minutes   **Makes:** 1 (13-inch) thin-crust pizza

	all-purpose flour
1	portion hand-tossed pizza dough, at room temperature (see recipe, page 24)
1	tablespoon extra-virgin olive oil
	kosher salt
⅓	cup Neapolitan pizza sauce (see recipe, page 116)
½	cup shredded mozzarella cheese
2	tablespoons grated Parmesan cheese
4	ounces Burrata cheese, torn into 1-inch pieces
6	to 8 whole small basil leaves

1 Preheat oven to 500°F. If using a baking stone, arrange a rack in the upper third of the oven and place stone on rack. Heat for 1 hour. (If using a baking sheet, arrange rack in middle of oven.)

2 On a lightly floured surface, roll dough portion to a 13-inch circle. Lightly sprinkle a pizza peel or rimless baking sheet with flour. Transfer the dough circle to prepared peel. (If using a baking sheet, lightly flour the baking sheet. Transfer dough circle to prepared sheet.)

3 Drizzle the 1 tablespoon olive oil over the dough. Use a pastry brush to distribute oil evenly over dough. Sprinkle very lightly with kosher salt. Spread Neapolitan pizza sauce on crust, leaving a ½ inch border around the edge. Distribute mozzarella and Parmesan evenly over the sauce.

4 Using small, quick back-and-forth movements, slide pizza from peel onto hot pizza stone. (If using a baking sheet, place sheet on rack in oven.)

5 Bake, rotating pizza halfway through baking time, until bottom of crust is crisp and top is blistered, 5 to 7 minutes.*

6 Remove from oven; immediately distribute Burrata and basil leaves over hot pizza. Serve immediately.

*tip Do not pop any bubbles that form on the dough.

california club pizza

Eat your pizza and salad all at once with this fork-and-knife pie that features all the elements of the classic club sandwich – chicken, bacon, tomato, lettuce, and avocado.

Prep: 30 minutes   **Bake:** 6 minutes per pizza   **Makes:** 2 (11-inch) pizzas

	all-purpose flour
2	portions hand-tossed pizza dough, at room temperature (see recipe, page 24)
2	cups shredded mozzarella cheese
6	ounces grilled chicken breast, pulled into ¼-inch-thick slices
4	slices thick-cut applewood-smoked bacon, crisp-cooked and broken into large pieces
2	cups torn romaine lettuce
2	cups baby arugula
6	large basil leaves, torn into 1½-inch pieces
2	tablespoons lemon-pepper mayo (see recipe, below)
1	large heirloom tomato, cut into ¼-inch-thick slices
1	avocado, cut into 12 slices

1 Preheat oven to 500°F. If using a baking stone, arrange a rack in the upper third of the oven and place stone on rack. Heat for 1 hour. (If using a baking sheet, arrange rack in middle of oven.)

2 Lightly flour a work surface. Place one portion of dough on the surface, being careful to maintain the round shape and thickness of the dough; do not press. Lightly flour the top of the dough. Using your index fingers, press a 1-inch rim around the outer edge of the circle. Once rim is formed, press air out of the center of the dough, being careful not to flatten the rim. Using your knuckles, from the bottom of the dough, carefully stretch the dough, rotating as you work, to form an 11-inch circle. Take care to maintain a uniform thickness in the center. Gently toss dough in the air a few times. Set aside and repeat with remaining ball of dough. Lightly sprinkle a pizza peel or rimless baking sheet with flour. Transfer one dough circle to prepared peel. (If using a baking sheet, lightly flour the baking sheet. Transfer one dough circle to prepared sheet.)

3 Top the dough circle on peel with 1 cup mozzarella, half of the chicken, and half of the bacon.

4 Using small, quick back-and-forth movements, slide pizza from peel onto hot pizza stone. (If using a baking sheet, place sheet on rack in oven.) Bake, rotating pizza halfway through baking time, until bottom of crust is crisp and top is blistered, 6 to 8 minutes.

5 While pizza is baking, combine romaine lettuce, arugula, basil leaves, and lemon-pepper mayo in a large bowl. Toss well to combine. When pizza is done baking, slice and top with half of the tomato slices and half of the lettuce mixture. Top with 6 slices of avocado; serve immediately. Repeat with remaining dough circle and toppings.

lemon-pepper mayo In a small bowl combine ½ cup mayonnaise, 1 tablespoon fresh lemon juice, and ½ teaspoon coarsely ground black pepper. Stir well to combine. Store in a tightly sealed container in the refrigerator. (Use leftover mayo as a sandwich spread or salad dressing.)

shrimp and grits with grilled sweet corn

Although this Southern standard of cheesy grits topped with a pile of spicy Cajun shrimp originated as a Lowcountry fisherman's breakfast, it was transformed into a very popular supper dish when a *New York Times* food writer did a story about it in the 1980s. These grits are studded with grilled corn, and the shrimp is bathed in a white wine-butter pan sauce.

Prep: 30 minutes   **Cook:** 15 minutes   **Makes:** 4 servings

grits

2	cups water
½	cup grits
1	tablespoon butter
2	teaspoons Crystal Hot Sauce or 1 teaspoon Tabasco (see tip, page 16)
½	cup shredded Monterey Jack cheese
½	cup shredded Cheddar cheese
¼	teaspoon salt
¼	teaspoon coarsely ground black pepper
	grilled sweet corn (see recipe, below right)

shrimp

1	tablespoon olive oil
1	pound extra-large shrimp, peeled, deveined, tails on
2	cloves garlic, minced
1	tablespoon Cajun blackening spice*
½	cup dry white wine
1	tablespoon freshly squeezed lemon juice
½	teaspoon kosher salt
2	tablespoons unsalted butter, cut into chunks
⅓	cup thinly sliced scallions (bias cut)

1 For grits, bring the water to a boil in a medium saucepan. Gradually whisk in grits. Reduce heat to low. Cover and cook until thickened, 10 to 12 minutes, stirring occasionally. Stir in butter, hot sauce, cheeses, salt, and pepper. Gently stir in grilled sweet corn kernels. Cover and keep warm.

2 Meanwhile, for shrimp, heat olive oil in a large sauté pan over medium heat. Add shrimp, garlic, and Cajun spice; sauté until shrimp are turning pink and nearly cooked, about 2 minutes.

3 Add wine and lemon juice; stir, scraping up any browned bits. Season with salt and add butter, swirling pan until butter is melted.

4 To serve, divide grits among four shallow bowls. Top each serving of grits with shrimp. Drizzle shrimp with pan sauce. Garnish with scallions and serve immediately.

grilled sweet corn Heat a charcoal or gas grill to medium-high. Shuck one ear of corn. Rinse and dry. Place directly over heat and cook, turning occasionally, until lightly charred on all sides and tender, about 10 to 12 minutes. Remove from grill; cool completely. (Alternatively, use a grill pan.) Using a sharp knife, cut down the sides of the ear to remove kernels. One ear yields between ¾ and 1 cup kernels.

*tip If the Cajun blackening spice you use contains salt, omit the ½ teaspoon kosher salt.

Holsteins range freely on a dairy farm outside Appleton, Wisconsin.
The black-and-white beauties are prized for their prolific milk production –
much of which is turned into cheese. Cheese is so important to pizza,
so we seek out the best quality we can get – and not surprisingly, that
comes from The Dairy State.

fire-grilled ribeye with roasted potato salad and oven-dried tomatoes

At CPK, we believe that you don't need to do much to prepare a great steak. Just season and cook it right, and that's all it really needs to be perfect. The only embellishment we offer this smoky grilled ribeye is a sprinkling of black pepper and homemade Pinot sea salt. The recipe itself is simple – it just takes a little planning. The wine-flavor salt needs to be made at least a day ahead, and the sweet oven-dried tomatoes take 4 hours to roast.

Prep: 20 minutes   **Bake:** 4 hours   **Grill:** 10 minutes   **Makes:** 4 servings

4   cups crispy roasted fingerling potatoes (see recipe, page 117), at room temperature
2   cups arugula
⅓   cup crumbled goat cheese
4   8-ounce boneless beef ribeye steaks, cut ¾ to 1 inch thick
2   teaspoons Pinot sea salt (see recipe, below)
    ground black pepper
¼   cup tarragon vinaigrette (see recipe, page 117)
    oven-dried tomatoes (see recipe, below)

1 Heat a charcoal or gas grill to medium-high.

2 In a large bowl combine crispy roasted fingerling potatoes, arugula, and goat cheese; set aside.

3 Place steaks on the hot grill. Sprinkle each steak with ¼ teaspoon Pinot sea salt and black pepper to taste. Turn and season each steak with remaining ¼ teaspoon Pinot sea salt and black pepper to taste. Grill to desired temperature, from rare to well done. Remove from grill and lightly cover with foil. Let rest for 5 minutes.

4 While steaks are resting, toss potato mixture with tarragon vinaigrette. Divide potato salad among four dinner plates. Place a steak and five tomato halves on each plate.

pinot sea salt In a small saucepan bring 1 cup Pinot Noir to boiling over medium-high heat. Lower to medium and boil until reduced to 1 tablespoon, about 25 minutes; cool slightly. In a bowl mix reduced wine and ½ cup coarse-grain sea salt until blended. Immediately spread onto a rimmed baking sheet in a thin layer and dry at room temperature, uncovered, overnight. Store in a tightly sealed container at room temperature for up to 3 weeks. Use to season meats and vegetables.

oven-dried tomatoes Preheat oven to 200°F. Cut 10 Roma tomatoes in half lengthwise. In a large bowl toss tomato halves with 1 tablespoon extra virgin olive oil and ½ teaspoon dried oregano. Arrange tomato halves, cut sides up, on a large rimmed baking sheet. Season to taste with kosher salt and black pepper. Roast for 4 hours or until tomatoes feel dry to the touch but are still slightly moist and chewy.

strawberry shortcake
with candied basil

This is the essence of summer on a dessert plate. Perfectly ripe, lightly sweetened strawberries are tucked into a tender, sugar-crusted biscuit and topped with whipped cream, ice cream, and a confetti of sugared basil, which adds a spark of color and brightness to this summertime treat.

Prep: 45 minutes   **Stand:** 3 hours   **Bake:** 18 minutes   **Makes:** 6 servings

biscuits

2½	cups all-purpose flour
3½	teaspoons baking powder
2	teaspoons sugar
¾	teaspoon kosher salt
¾	cup heavy cream
½	cup whole milk
	coarse sugar (decorating sugar)

strawberries

4	cups sliced strawberries
3	tablespoons sugar
1	cup pureed strawberries
½	teaspoon vanilla extract

to serve

2	cups vanilla ice cream
1½	cups sweetened whipped cream (see recipe, below) candied basil (see recipe, below)

1 Heat oven to 375°F. For the biscuits, line a large rimmed baking sheet with parchment paper. In a large mixing bowl combine flour, baking powder, sugar, and salt. In a small bowl combine cream and milk. Slowly pour milk mixture into dry mixture, stirring gently to combine, just until dough comes together.

2 Scoop dough onto parchment-lined baking sheet in six equal mounds. Sprinkle each with about ½ teaspoon coarse sugar. Bake until light golden brown and set, and a toothpick comes out clean, about 18 to 22 minutes; let cool on a wire rack.

3 While biscuits are baking, combine sliced strawberries, sugar, pureed strawberries, and vanilla in a medium bowl. Toss to combine; set aside.

4 To serve, cut biscuits in half horizontally. If necessary, warm in the microwave for 20 to 30 seconds. Place bottom halves in serving dishes. Divide strawberries among the biscuit bottoms, drizzling each with additional strawberry puree. Place a scoop of vanilla ice cream on top of strawberries. Top with a dollop of sweetened whipped cream. Sprinkle with candied basil. Place biscuit top at an angle, leaning off one side of the whipped cream. Serve immediately.

sweetened whipped cream To make 1½ cups sweetened whipped cream, combine ¾ cup heavy whipping cream, 2 teaspoons granulated sugar, and ¼ teaspoon vanilla extract in a chilled medium bowl. Whisk or beat with an electric mixer on low speed until soft peaks form.

candied basil In a small bowl combine 2 tablespoons granulated sugar and 2 teaspoons very finely chopped fresh basil. Whisk to thoroughly coat. Spread mixture in a thin layer on a small rimmed baking pan. Allow to dry at room temperature for 3 to 4 hours or until mixture is dried, stirring occasionally to ensure even drying.

cucumber-basil soda

This delectably light, not overly sweet, grown-up soda has hints of cucumber and basil – and lots of refreshing bubbles.

Prep: 5 minutes   **Cook:** 5 minutes   **Stand:** 30 minutes   **Makes:** 12 servings

1   cup granulated sugar
1   cup water
1   medium cucumber, thinly sliced
12 large basil leaves
9   cups soda water, chilled
    ice
    cucumber slices and fresh basil leaves, for garnish

1 In a medium saucepan combine sugar and the water over medium heat. Cook, stirring occasionally, until sugar is dissolved and mixture just comes to a boil, about 5 minutes.

2 In a small bowl muddle the cucumber and 12 basil leaves with the back of a wooden spoon. Add to the hot syrup. Cover and let steep for 30 minutes. Strain the syrup, pressing the solids through a fine-mesh strainer to release the flavors. Discard solids.

3 For each serving, combine 3 tablespoons of the syrup with ¾ cup soda water in an ice-filled glass. Stir gently to combine. Garnish with cucumber slices and a basil leaf.

note Cucumber-basil syrup can be stored in a tightly sealed container in the refrigerator for up to 3 days.

california roots

The surprise ingredient in this vodka cocktail sweetened with agave is avocado, which imparts body and a beautiful verdant color. The fennel salt rim is incredibly fragrant and truly enhances every sip.

Start to finish: 15 minutes   **Makes:** 1 drink

    lime wedge
    fennel salt (see recipe, below)
1½ ounces vodka
1   ounce fresh agave sour (see recipe, page 114)
½   ounce agave nectar
¼   of a ripe avocado, mashed
    ice
    mint sprig

Run the lime wedge around half of the rim of a 6- or 8-ounce old-fashioned glass. Spread some fennel salt on a small plate or shallow dish. Dip moistened half of rim in salt. Fill glass with ice. Fill a cocktail shaker with ice; add vodka, fresh agave sour, agave nectar, and avocado. Cover and shake vigorously, until avocado is completely incorporated into mixture. Strain into prepared glass. Garnish with mint sprig and serve immediately.

fennel salt In an electric spice grinder or clean coffee bean grinder combine 1 tablespoon kosher salt and 1 tablespoon fennel seeds. Blend until fennel seeds are coarsely ground, about 5 seconds. Store at room temperature in an airtight container.

fall

As temperatures cool, the air turns crisp, and so does the array of peak-season produce. Hearty greens, crunchy Brussels sprouts, apples, and firm, ripe pears take center stage. The earthy smell of rain-dampened leaves is mirrored in the aroma of wild mushrooms and olive oil pressed just after harvest.

harvest kale salad

Farro is an ancient Italian grain related to wheat. When toasted, it reveals a deliciously nutty flavor. Cubes of sweet caramelized butternut squash are a pleasant surprise in this autumnal salad of farro, kale, napa cabbage, thinly sliced pear, spiced toasted pecans, and tart dried cranberries.

Start to finish: 20 minutes   **Makes:** 2 main-dish servings or 4 side-dish servings

4	cups baby kale
3	cups finely shredded napa cabbage
1	cup roasted butternut squash (see recipe, page 118)
⅔	cup toasted farro, cooked and cooled (see recipe, page 108)
1	medium ripe pear, cored, quartered, and thinly sliced
¼	cup dried cranberries
½	cup spiced toasted pecans (see recipe, right)
⅓	cup citrus vinaigrette (see recipe, below)
¼	cup crumbled goat cheese

1 In a large bowl combine kale, cabbage, roasted butternut squash, farro, pear, cranberries, spiced toasted pecans, and citrus vinaigrette. Toss gently to combine.

2 Divide among two large or four small chilled plates, making sure all ingredients are evenly distributed throughout each serving. Sprinkle with goat cheese; serve immediately.

spiced toasted pecans Preheat oven to 350°F. In a small mixing bowl combine 1 tablespoon sugar, ½ teaspoon salt, and 1 teaspoon smoked paprika; set aside. In a medium bowl combine 2 cups pecan halves and 2 tablespoons refrigerated egg whites. Toss until pecans are well coated. Sprinkle with spice mixture while tossing gently. Spread nuts on a large rimmed baking pan. Bake for 10 minutes. Gently stir and bake for 2 to 3 minutes more. Remove from oven and let cool completely on a wire rack. Store nuts in a tightly sealed container at room temperature for up to 3 days. Makes 2 cups.

citrus vinaigrette In a blender container combine ¼ cup freshly squeezed lemon juice, ½ cup extra virgin olive oil, 1½ teaspoons Dijon mustard, ¼ teaspoon salt, and ¼ teaspoon ground cayenne pepper. Blend on high for 30 seconds or until smooth and emulsified. Store in a covered container in the refrigerator for up to 5 days. Makes about 1 cup.

korean sweet chili wings

The combination of sweet and heat is irresistible in these battered-and-glazed Asian-style wings. The sweet chili sauce can be made a few hours ahead and then carefully reheated right before serving.

Prep: 1 hour 30 minutes   **Chill:** 30 minutes   **Cook:** 5 minutes per batch   **Makes:** 4 to 6 servings

marinade

- 3 tablespoons minced fresh ginger
- 2 tablespoons sambal oelek (Indonesian chili paste)
- 2 teaspoons kosher salt
- ½ teaspoon ground white pepper
- 2 pounds chicken wing drummettes

batter

- vegetable oil, for frying
- ¼ cup all-purpose flour
- ¼ cup cornstarch
- ½ teaspoon baking powder
- ½ cup cold water
- 1 egg white

to serve

- 1 recipe sweet chili sauce (see recipe, below)
- ½ cup julienned scallions
- ⅓ cup fresh cilantro leaves
- ¼ cup roughly chopped dry-roasted peanuts

1 For marinade, in a large bowl combine ginger, sambal oelek, salt, and white pepper. Stir until smooth. Add chicken drummettes to bowl. Using your hands, toss until all chicken pieces are well coated. Cover bowl with plastic wrap and refrigerate for 30 minutes to 1 hour.

2 Fill a large, tall pot with 2 inches of vegetable oil. Insert a thermometer and heat oil to 350°F.

3 For batter, combine flour, cornstarch, and baking powder in a medium bowl. In a small bowl whisk together the water and egg white. Whisk egg white mixture into dry mixture until smooth.

4 Preheat oven to 200°F. Working in batches, dip chicken in batter, turning to coat fully, and carefully add to the hot oil. Cook 5 to 7 minutes or until golden brown and chicken is cooked through. (Be sure to allow oil to come back up to 350°F between batches.) Drain chicken on a large rimmed baking sheet lined with paper towels. (Keep cooked chicken warm in the oven.)

5 When ready to serve, toss cooked chicken with ¾ cup of the warm sweet chili sauce (including the toasted chilies) in a large bowl. Transfer chicken to a serving platter. Top with scallions, cilantro, and peanuts. Serve immediately with remaining sweet chili sauce for dipping.

sweet chili sauce In a medium skillet heat 1 tablespoon canola oil and 10 dried red Thai chiles over medium heat about 2 minutes or until chiles darken and oil is infused with flavor, stirring occasionally. Remove from heat; add 1½ cups packed light brown sugar, ½ cup soy sauce, ¼ cup apple cider vinegar, and 1 tablespoon minced fresh ginger. Bring to a boil, stirring constantly. Reduce heat, uncover, and simmer 10 minutes or until sauce just starts to thicken, stirring occasionally. Keep sauce warm until ready to serve.

wild mushroom pizza

Use any combination of mushrooms you can find on this luxurious pizza. Shiitakes add an intensely rich, buttery flavor to foods – and they're readily available. The drizzle of truffle oil is optional but takes this pizza over the top. It is expensive, but a little goes a very long way.

Prep: 30 minutes   **Bake:** 6 minutes per pizza   **Makes:** 2 (11-inch) pizzas

2   tablespoons extra virgin olive oil

1   clove garlic, minced all-purpose flour

2   portions hand-tossed pizza dough, at room temperature (see recipe, page 24)

1   cup shredded mozzarella cheese

¼   cup shaved Romano cheese

2   cups thinly sliced mixed mushrooms, such as shiitake (stemmed), cremini, and portobello

1   cup thinly sliced fresh chanterelle mushrooms

3   tablespoons grated Parmesan cheese, divided

1   teaspoon cracked black pepper

¼   cup julienned scallions

1   teaspoon white truffle oil (optional)

1 Preheat oven to 500°F. If using a baking stone, arrange a rack in the upper third of the oven and place stone on rack. Heat for 1 hour. (If using a baking sheet, arrange rack in middle of oven.)

2 In a small bowl combine olive oil and garlic; set aside.

3 Lightly flour a work surface. Place one portion of dough on the surface, being careful to maintain the round shape and thickness of the dough; do not press. Lightly flour the top of the dough. Using your index fingers, press a 1-inch rim around the outer edge of the circle. Once rim is formed, press air out of the center of the dough, being careful not to flatten the rim. Using your knuckles, from the bottom of the dough, carefully stretch the dough, rotating as you work, to form an 11-inch circle. Take care to maintain a uniform thickness in the center. Gently toss dough in the air a few times. Set aside and repeat with remaining ball of dough. Lightly sprinkle a pizza peel or rimless baking sheet with flour. Transfer one dough circle to prepared peel. (If using a baking sheet, lightly flour the baking sheet. Transfer one dough circle to prepared sheet.)

4 Brush about 1 tablespoon of the garlic-infused oil over the dough circle on peel, making sure any pieces of minced garlic are evenly distributed, avoiding the rim. Sprinkle with half of the mozzarella and half of the Romano. Top with half of the mixed mushrooms and half of the chanterelles. Sprinkle with 1 tablespoon of the grated Parmesan, ½ teaspoon of the cracked black pepper, and 2 tablespoons of the scallions.

5 Using small, quick back-and-forth movements, slide pizza from peel onto hot pizza stone. (If using a baking sheet, place sheet on rack in oven.)

6 Bake, rotating pizza halfway through baking time, until bottom of crust is crisp and top is blistered, 6 to 8 minutes.* If desired, drizzle with ½ teaspoon truffle oil. Sprinkle with 1½ teaspoons grated Parmesan. Repeat with remaining dough circle, garlic oil, and toppings.

*tip Do not pop any bubbles that form on the dough.

Mount Shasta provides a stunning backdrop to rows of olive trees at the California Olive Ranch north of Sacramento. CPK uses olive oil produced by California Olive Ranch exclusively because of its amazing quality and freshness.

brussels sprouts and bacon flatbreads

The Brussels sprouts are peeled into pretty individual leaves for this flatbread that is also topped with caramelized onions, bacon, and three cheeses: goat cheese, Parmesan, and Romano.

Prep: 30 minutes **Bake:** 6 minutes per flatbread **Makes:** 4 (12×4-inch) flatbreads

2   ounces creamy goat cheese, softened

¼   cup heavy cream

1   teaspoon Dijon mustard
    all-purpose flour

2   portions hand-tossed pizza dough, at room temperature (see recipe, page 24)

¼   cup shaved Romano cheese
    caramelized onions (see recipe, page 118)

4   slices thick-cut bacon, crisp-cooked and broken into large pieces

3   cups Brussels sprouts leaves*

1   tablespoon extra virgin olive oil

½   teaspoon cracked black pepper

¼   cup grated Parmesan cheese, divided

1 Heat oven to 500°F. If using a baking stone, arrange a rack in the upper third of the oven and place stone on rack. Heat for 1 hour. (If using a baking sheet, arrange rack in middle of oven.)

2 In a small bowl mix together goat cheese, cream, and mustard; set aside.

3 On a lightly floured surface, cut one portion of dough in half. Working with one half at a time, shape into a rough oval. Using a rolling pin, roll dough into a long, narrow oval, approximately 12×4 inches. Lightly sprinkle a pizza peel or rimless baking sheet with flour. Transfer dough oval to prepared peel.

4 Use the back of a spoon to evenly spread one-fourth of the goat cheese mixture on dough oval, leaving a ¼-inch border around the edge. Sprinkle with 1 tablespoon Romano cheese. Top with one-fourth of the caramelized onions and one-fourth of the bacon.

5 In a medium bowl toss Brussels sprouts leaves with olive oil and cracked black pepper. Top flatbread with one-fourth of the Brussels sprouts leaves. Sprinkle with a generous teaspoon of Parmesan.

6 Using small, quick back-and-forth movements, slide flatbread from peel onto hot pizza stone. (If using a baking sheet, place sheet on rack in oven.) Bake until crust and Brussels sprouts leaves are lightly charred, about 6 to 8 minutes, popping bubbles with a spoon as needed.

7 Cut flatbread on the bias into four slices. Sprinkle with some of the remaining Parmesan and serve immediately. Repeat with remaining dough and toppings.

*tip To prepare the Brussels sprouts, cut off core and gently break apart heads into individual leaves.

chicken tequila pasta

Two favorite cuisines – Italian and Mexican - blend together beautifully in this creamy and colorful dish made with a trio of sweet peppers. If you can't find dried spinach pasta, regular fettuccine works just fine.

Prep: 30 minutes   **Cook:** 25 minutes   **Makes:** 6 to 8 servings

1   pound dried spinach or regular fettuccine
4   garlic cloves, minced
1   large jalapeño, seeded and minced
½   cup chopped fresh cilantro
6   tablespoons unsalted butter
½   cup chicken stock or broth
2   tablespoons gold tequila
2   tablespoons freshly squeezed lime juice
1½ pounds boneless, skinless chicken breast, cut into ½ inch dice
3   tablespoons soy sauce
¼   of a medium red onion, thinly sliced
½   of a medium red bell pepper, thinly sliced
½   of a medium yellow bell pepper, thinly sliced
½   of a medium green bell pepper, thinly sliced
1   cup heavy whipping cream
    kosher salt
    freshly ground black pepper
    lime wedges, for garnish

1 Cook pasta according to package directions to al dente, about 8 to 10 minutes. Drain pasta, reserving some of the cooking water.

2 Meanwhile, in a small sauté pan cook garlic, jalapeño, and ⅓ cup of the cilantro in 2 tablespoons of the butter over medium heat for 4 to 5 minutes. Add chicken stock, tequila, and lime juice. Bring to a boil and reduce to a pastelike consistency. Set aside.

3 In a medium bowl combine chicken and soy sauce; toss to evenly coat. Set aside to marinate.

4 While chicken is marinating, cook onion and bell peppers in remaining 4 tablespoons butter in a large sauté pan over medium heat until vegetables have wilted and start to brown, about 5 to 6 minutes. Add chicken and soy sauce liquid, reserved tequila lime paste, and cream.

5 Bring sauce to a boil and simmer until chicken is cooked and cream thickens, about 5 minutes. Add drained pasta and remaining cilantro. Season to taste with salt and pepper. Toss until well combined. Garnish with lime wedges and serve immediately.

CPK chefs Brian Sullivan (left) and Paul Pszybylski (right) take in the beauty of the olive orchards at California Olive Ranch during the fall harvest and tasting. California Olive Ranch produces several types of olive oil, including an extra virgin oil made exclusively from Arbequina olives, shown here.

california olive oil cake

In olive-producing countries such as Italy, Portugal, and Spain, it is common practice to make sweet cakes with olive oil instead of butter. We developed this recipe as a way to showcase the wonderful olive oil produced by California Olive Ranch (see pages 76–77 and 80–81). This cake is lovely served plain or with seasonal fruit.

Prep: 20 minutes   **Bake:** 25 minutes   **Cool:** 15 minutes   **Makes:** 8 to 10 servings

1   tablespoon butter, softened
2   tablespoons coarse sugar (decorating sugar)
1   cup granulated sugar
3   large eggs
¾   cup extra virgin olive oil
1   cup milk
⅓   cup pear juice
2   teaspoons grated lemon zest
1   teaspoon vanilla extract
2   cups all-purpose flour
½   teaspon kosher salt
½   teaspoon baking powder
½   teaspoon baking soda
½   cup sliced almonds
     powdered sugar (optional)

1 Preheat oven to 350°F. Brush a 9×9-inch cake pan with softened butter. Add coarse sugar to pan, and gently shake and turn until the pan is coated. Tap out excess sugar.

2 In a large mixing bowl, combine granulated sugar, eggs, olive oil, milk, pear juice, lemon zest, and vanilla extract. Beat on medium speed with an electric mixer for 1 minute or until ingredients are well blended.

3 In a separate bowl, whisk together flour, salt, baking powder, and baking soda. Slowly add dry ingredients to the wet mixture, mixing on low speed just until ingredients are well combined, about 1 to 2 minutes.

4 Pour batter into prepared pan. Sprinkle with sliced almonds. Bake 25 to 30 minutes or until a cake tester or toothpick inserted into the center comes out clean.

5 Cool cake in pan on a wire rack for at least 15 minutes. If desired, dust cake with powdered sugar. Serve warm or at room temperature.

roasted garlic chicken with fall vegetables

This recipe takes a bit of time to make, but as the chicken roasts and fills your home with warm and wonderful smells, and then emerges from the oven with a crackling crisp skin, you'll know it was worth the effort.

Prep: 1 hour 30 minutes   **Roast:** 40 minutes   **Makes:** 4 servings

vegetables

2 cups large cauliflower florets

2 tablespoons olive oil
kosher salt
ground black pepper

2 cups halved fingerling potatoes

2 cups halved Brussels sprouts
caramelized onions (see recipe, page 118)

2 tablespoons California olive oil with Mediterranean herbs (see recipe, opposite)

¼ cup chopped fresh Italian parsley

chicken

1 tablespoon unsalted butter

1 tablespoon olive oil

4 chicken breast halves, deboned with skin (2½ to 3 pounds total)*
kosher salt
ground black pepper

sauce

2 tablespoons chopped roasted garlic (see recipe, page 118)

¾ cup dry white wine (Chablis or Chardonnay)

4 teaspoons soy sauce

4 teaspoons lemon juice

½ teaspoon cracked black pepper

8 tablespoons unsalted butter

¼ cup chopped fresh Italian parsley

1 Preheat oven to 450°F.

2 In a medium bowl toss cauliflower with 2 teaspoons of the olive oil. Season with salt and pepper. Spread in a single layer in a 15×10×1-inch baking pan. Roast in the oven for 5 minutes. In the same bowl toss potatoes with 2 teaspoons of the olive oil. Season with salt and pepper. Add to baking pan with cauliflower, stirring to combine vegetables. Roast for 5 minutes. In the same bowl combine halved Brussels sprouts with remaining 2 teaspoons olive oil. Season with salt and pepper. Add to baking pan with cauliflower and potatoes, stirring to combine vegetables. Continue to roast for about 30 minutes or until vegetables are crisp-tender, and well browned, stirring once halfway through roasting.

3 Meanwhile, for chicken, heat a large skillet over medium-high heat. Add butter and olive oil to pan. Pat chicken dry with a paper towel and season with salt and pepper. Lay chicken skin side down in the skillet and cook undisturbed until skin is golden and crispy, about 4 minutes. Turn chicken and cook until opaque, about 4 minutes more. Transfer chicken to a 2-quart

rectangular baking dish. Roast in the oven alongside vegetables until chicken breast reaches 160°F, about 10 to 12 minutes. Take chicken out of the oven and let rest loosely covered with aluminum foil, for 5 minutes.

4 For lemon-garlic sauce, while chicken is roasting, drain all but 1 tablespoon drippings from skillet. Heat chopped roasted garlic in drippings over medium heat, stirring constantly for about 1 minute. Remove from heat; carefully add white wine, soy sauce, lemon juice, and black pepper to pan. Return to medium heat; cook and stir, scraping up any browned bits. Add butter, 1 tablespoon at a time, whisking constantly until smooth. Allow each addition to melt before adding the next one. Stir in parsley and remove from heat.

5 Remove vegetables from the oven. Add caramelized onions to baking pan and toss to combine with vegetables. Drizzle vegetables with California olive oil with Mediterranean herbs and sprinkle with parsley. Toss to combine.

6 To serve, divide vegetables among four shallow bowls. Slice each chicken breast at a 45° angle and stack chicken breast, skin side up, on the center of the vegetables. Spoon lemon-garlic sauce over vegetables and chicken.

*tip To debone a chicken breast half, place the breast skin side down on a cutting board. Slide the blade of a thin, sharp knife along the breastbone, angling the cutting edge slightly into the bone to avoid nicking the flesh. Use short, swiping strokes. Slide the blade under the rib bones and work toward the outer edge of the breast until the ribs and breastbone are free. With the tip of the knife, cut around the shoulder joint where the wing had been attached to the breast. Feel with your fingers along the top edge of the breast for half of the wishbone. Free the tip of that bone with the tip of your knife. Holding the bone tip in one hand, scrape bone with the knife to free it, working back toward the joint where the wishbone connects to the ribs. Cut through the connective tissue holding the bone to the meat and pull off the ribs and wishbone together. Trim the thin flap of rib meat to neaten the breast. Turn breast over and trim any straggly pieces of meat. Smooth the skin.

california olive oil with mediterranean herbs In a bowl combine ½ cup extra virgin olive oil; 1½ teaspoons very finely chopped fresh basil; 1½ teaspoons very finely chopped Italian parsley; ⅛ teaspoon dried thyme, crushed; ⅛ teaspoon kosher salt; ⅛ teaspoon dried oregano, crushed; ⅛ teaspoon garlic powder; and a dash of crushed red chile flakes. Stir to combine. Store at room temperature for up to 2 days.** Stir before using.

**tip Toss roasted or steamed vegetables with leftover flavored oil, use it as a dipping sauce for bread, or use it to make your favorite vinaigrette.

fresh pomegranate lemonade

Pomegranates are in season from early fall to early winter. You can buy the whole fruit and remove the seeds yourself, or buy them already removed from the rind. Small containers of the seeds, or arils, are available in the produce section of many supermarkets.

Start to finish: 10 minutes   **Makes:** 6 servings

1   cup pomegranate juice, chilled
4   cups lemonade, chilled
4   cups lemon-lime soda, chilled
     ice
6   tablespoons pomegranate arils

In a large pitcher combine pomegranate juice, lemonade, and soda. Stir gently to combine. Divide among four 12-ounce ice-filled glasses. Top each serving with 1 tablespoon pomegranate arils. Serve immediately.

citrus adobo margarita

A tiny bit of chipotle in adobo sauce adds spice and subtle smokiness to this refreshing and unusual margarita.

Start to Finish: 10 minutes   **Makes:** 1 drink

2   lime wedges
     kosher salt
1½   ounces tequila blanco
½   ounce Cointreau (orange-flavor liqueur)
¼   teaspoon chipotle in adobo sauce, minced
1½   ounces fresh agave sour (see recipe, page 114)
     ice
1   orange wedge
     lime slice

Run one of the lime wedges around half of the rim of an old-fashioned glass; discard lime wedge. Spread some kosher salt on a small plate or shallow dish. Dip moistened half of rim in salt. In a cocktail shaker combine tequila, Cointreau, chipotle in adobo, and fresh agave sour. Fill shaker with ice. Cover and shake vigorously. Squeeze the remaining lime wedge and the orange wedge into the prepared glass; discard peels. Pour drink into prepared glass (do not strain). Add more ice to glass if necessary. Garnish with lime slice and serve immediately.

winter

In the chill of a midwinter's day, appetites turn to heartier fare, and nature complies. Hardy vegetables such as beets, cabbages, potatoes, leeks, and squash – as well as crimson pomegranate seeds – bring deep jewel tones to favorite dishes. Soups and ragus provide a warmth and comfort that challenge the season's coldness, as do warm drinks that are perfect for sipping by the fireplace after a day spent outdoors in the bracing weather.

roasted beet salad with whipped goat cheese

Two varieties of beets give this knife-and-fork salad its earthy flavor and eye-catching color. Be sure to dip each bite in the herbed goat cheese.

Prep: 20 minutes   **Roast:** 35 minutes   **Makes:** 4 side-dish servings

1   recipe whipped goat cheese (see recipe, below)
1   recipe roasted beets (see recipe, below)
3   stalks celery, trimmed and bias-cut into ¼-inch slices
6   cups watercress
⅓   cup fresh Italian parsley leaves
⅓   cup lemon-herb vinaigrette (see recipe, page 116)
2   tablespoons coarsely chopped pistachios

1 Spread one-fourth of the whipped goat cheese on each of four chilled salad plates.

2 In a large bowl, combine the roasted golden beets, celery, watercress, parsley, and lemon-herb vinaigrette. Toss until well combined. Divide among four prepared salad plates. Place red beets in bowl and toss with any remaining dressing. Divide red beets among salads. Top with pistachios. Serve immediately.

whipped goat cheese In a small bowl, combine 4 ounces softened goat cheese, 3 tablespoons milk, and ¼ teaspoon cracked black pepper. Using a rubber spatula, vigorously stir mixture until well combined, scraping sides of bowl frequently. Add 2 teaspoons minced fresh herbs such as parsley or basil. Stir vigorously until smooth.

roasted beets Preheat oven to 450°F. Trim ¼ inch off both ends of 1 medium golden beet. Peel with a vegetable peeler. Stand beet on a flat end and cut into eight wedges. Repeat with 1 medium red beet. (Work with the golden beet first, as red beets will stain the golden beet; keep beets separate while preparing and cooking.) Transfer beets to two separate bowls. Toss each beet with 1 teaspoon olive oil. Season each with kosher salt. Lay two large sheets of aluminum foil on a work surface. Place golden beets in a single layer on one sheet of foil and red beets on the other sheet. Fold sides of foil up over beets and seal edges. Place foil packets on a rimmed baking sheet. Roast beets for 35 to 40 minutes or until tender when pierced. Uncover and let cool completely. (This may be done up to 1 day ahead. Store cooled beets separately in a tightly sealed container in the refrigerator.)

posole rojo (red posole)

Toppings of shredded cabbage, red onion, shaved radishes, cilantro, and avocado add freshness to this traditional Mexican stew made with pork shoulder, hominy, and an amazing roasted red chile sauce. The long cooking time makes the pork shoulder meltingly tender.

Prep: 40 minutes   **Cook:** 2 hours   **Makes:** 4 to 6 servings

posole

14	cups low-sodium chicken broth (3 quarts plus 2 cups)
3	15-ounce cans white hominy, rinsed and drained
1½	pounds pork shoulder, trimmed and cut into 2-inch pieces*
1	large yellow onion, peeled and cut in half**
2	large heads garlic, loose skin removed and top trimmed ¼ inch
4	bay leaves
1	teaspoon dried Mexican oregano

roasted red chile sauce

8	dried guajuillo chiles, stemmed, seeded, and membranes removed***
5	dried morita chiles, stemmed, seeded, and membrane removed***
4	cups cold water
2	garlic cloves, peeled
¼	cup chopped onion
1	tablespoon chicken soup base

garnishes

2½	cups shredded green cabbage
½	cup diced red onion
½	cup shaved radishes
½	cup chopped fresh cilantro
1	avocado, peeled, seeded, and cut into ½-inch dice
1	lime, cut into wedges

1 For the posole, combine chicken broth and hominy in a stockpot. Bring to a boil. Cover; reduce heat to medium and boil for 30 minutes. Add pork shoulder (including any bones), halved yellow onion, garlic heads, bay leaves, and oregano. Bring to a boil. Cover; reduce heat to medium and cook for an additional 30 minutes.

2 Meanwhile, for roasted red chile sauce, toast dried chiles in batches in a large skillet over high heat until they turn dark brown but not black; set aside to cool.

3 In a large saucepan combine toasted chiles with the 4 cups cold water. Bring to a boil and cook for 1 minute; drain.

4 In a blender container combine softened chiles, garlic cloves, chopped onion, soup base, and 2 cups of the posole broth (after it has cooked the second 30 minutes). Blend until smooth. Strain through a medium-mesh strainer and discard solids.

5 Add chile sauce to posole broth. Cover and continue to cook for 1 hour or until pork is tender.

6 Use a slotted spoon to remove halved onion, garlic heads, bay leaves, and pork bones, if using; discard. Ladle posole into warmed shallow soup bowls. Top with cabbage, red onion, radishes, cilantro, and avocado. Serve with lime wedges.

*tip For the best flavor, simmer the posole with bones from the pork shoulder, if possible.

**tip Leave the root end of the onion intact so the onion will not fall apart during cooking.

***tip Dried guajillo and morita chiles can be found at Mexican grocers.

The winter sunlight reveals the rich greens and burgundies of the cabbage patch at Suzie's Farm, a 140-acre USDA-certified organic farm and CSA (Community-Supported Agriculture) north of San Diego

California Pizza Kitchen chefs look to organic farms and CSAs for not only the freshest and healthiest produce, but for new trends in vegetables and heirloom varieties they can use in creating new recipes.

mupesa pizza (mushroom, pepperoni, and sausage pizza)

Where did the name for this pizza come from? Easy! Put all the toppings together – mushroom ("mu"), pepperoni ("pe"), and sausage ("sa") – and you have a unique name and one very tasty pie!

Prep: 20 minutes   **Bake:** 6 minutes per pizza   **Makes:** 2 (11-inch) pizzas

all-purpose flour

2 portions hand-tossed pizza dough, at room temperature (see recipe, page 24)

6 tablespoons Neapolitan pizza sauce (see recipe, page 116)

2 cups shredded mozzarella cheese

12 whole large basil leaves

8 ounces spicy Italian sausage, cooked and drained

16 slices pepperoni

¾ cup thinly sliced cremini mushrooms

1 teaspoon dried Greek oregano, crushed

1 Preheat oven to 500°F. If using a baking stone, arrange a rack in the upper third of the oven and place stone on rack. Heat for 1 hour. (If using a baking sheet, arrange rack in middle of oven.)

2 Lightly flour a work surface. Place one portion of dough on the surface, being careful to maintain the round shape and thickness of the dough; do not press. Lightly flour the top of the dough. Using your index fingers, press a 1-inch rim around the outer edge of the circle. Once rim is formed, press air out of the center of the dough, being careful not to flatten the rim. Using your knuckles, from the bottom of the dough, carefully stretch the dough, rotating as you work, to form an 11-inch circle. Take care to maintain a uniform thickness in the center. Gently toss dough in the air a few times. Set aside and repeat with remaining ball of dough. Lightly sprinkle a pizza peel or rimless baking sheet with flour. Transfer one dough circle to prepared peel. (If using a baking sheet, lightly flour baking sheet. Transfer one dough circle to prepared sheet.)

3 Spread half of the Neapolitan pizza sauce on the dough circle on peel, avoiding the rim. Distribute half of the cheese evenly over the sauce. Top with half each of the basil leaves, sausage, pepperoni, and mushrooms.

4 Using small, quick back-and-forth movements, slide pizza from peel onto hot pizza stone. (If using a baking sheet, place sheet on rack in oven.)

5 Bake, rotating pizza halfway through baking time, until bottom of crust is crisp and top is blistered, 6 to 8 minutes.* Garnish with ½ teaspoon of the dried Greek oregano. Repeat with remaining dough circle, sauce, and toppings.

*tip Do not pop any bubbles that form.

sunny-side-up potato and bacon pizza

Although this egg-and-bacon-topped pie is perfect for brunch, it's equally delicious any time of the day. Be sure to cook the pizza just long enough so the egg yolks stay slightly runny.

Prep: 30 minutes   **Bake:** 6 minutes per pizza   **Makes:** 2 (11-inch) pizzas

4 slices thick-cut applewood-smoked bacon, cut into 2-inch pieces

1 small leek, cut in half lengthwise, bias-sliced into ½-inch slices, and washed (use whole leek with bruised leaves removed)*
   all-purpose flour

2 portions hand-tossed pizza dough, at room temperature (see recipe, page 24)

¼ cup shaved Parmesan cheese

1½ cups shredded mozzarella cheese

1 cup crispy roasted fingerling potatoes (see recipe, page 117)

4 large eggs
   kosher salt

½ teaspoon cracked black pepper

1 Preheat oven to 500°F. If using a baking stone, arrange a rack in the upper third of the oven and place stone on rack. Heat for 1 hour. (If using a baking sheet, arrange rack in middle of oven.)

2 In a medium skillet cook bacon over medium heat until crispy, about 8 minutes. Drain bacon on paper towels. Drain off all but about 1 tablespoon of drippings from pan. Add sliced leek. Sauté over low heat, stirring occasionally, until leek becomes soft and edges start to turn golden brown, about 5 minutes. Transfer to a plate to cool; set aside.

3 Lightly flour a work surface. Place one portion of dough on the surface, being careful to maintain the round shape and thickness of the dough; do not press. Lightly flour the top of the dough. Using your index fingers, press a 1-inch rim around the outer edge of the circle. Once rim is formed, press air out of the center of the dough, being careful not to flatten the rim. Using your knuckles, from the bottom of the dough, carefully stretch the dough, rotating as you work, to form an 11-inch circle. Take care to maintain a uniform thickness in the center. Gently toss dough in the air a few times. Set aside and repeat with remaining ball of dough. Lightly sprinkle a pizza peel or rimless baking sheet with flour. Transfer one dough circle to prepared peel. (If using a baking sheet, lightly flour the baking sheet. Transfer one dough circle to prepared sheet.)

4 Distribute half of the Parmesan and half of the mozzarella over the dough circle on peel, avoiding rim. Top with half each of the cooked bacon, crispy roasted fingerling potatoes, and leeks.

recipe continued on page 100

recipe continued from page 98

5 Crack one egg into a small dish. Gently transfer egg to one half of the pizza. Repeat with additional egg. Sprinkle each egg lightly with salt. Sprinkle ¼ teaspoon of the cracked black pepper over entire pizza.

6 Using small, quick back-and-forth movements, slide pizza from peel onto hot pizza stone, being careful not to break eggs. (If using a baking sheet, place sheet on rack in oven.)

7 Bake, rotating pizza halfway through baking time, until bottom of crust is crisp and top is blistered and egg whites are set (yolk should still be runny), 6 to 8 minutes.** Repeat with remaining dough circle and toppings.

*tip To wash leeks before using, place slices in a bowl of cold water, swirling to remove any sand or grit. Drain in a fine-mesh strainer and pat dry with paper towels.

**tip Do not pop any bubbles that form on the dough.

short rib ragu with cracked pepper pappardelle

This is very special Sunday supper food – a rich ragu of braised short ribs in tomato sauce splashed with cream and served over ribbons of pasta. If you don't have time to make your own pasta, you can certainly use prepared dried pappardelle.

Prep: 1 hour   **Cook:** 2 hours   **Makes:** 4 servings

short ribs

3	pounds beef short ribs
1	teaspoon kosher salt
2	teaspoons cracked black pepper
2	tablespoons olive oil
2	tablespoons butter
3	cups cold water
3	cups chicken stock or broth

ragu

2	tablespoons extra virgin olive oil
2	cloves garlic, peeled and very thinly sliced
1	cup pureed canned Italian tomatoes
1	cup reserved braising liquid
⅔	cup heavy whipping cream
1	tablespoon snipped fresh oregano

½	teaspoon kosher salt
½	teaspoon cracked black pepper

to serve

	cracked pepper pappardelle (see recipe, page 106)
1	tablespoon chopped fresh chives
¼	cup shaved Parmesan cheese

1   For the short ribs, preheat the oven to 350°F. Season ribs with salt and pepper.

2   Heat olive oil and butter in a Dutch oven or large skillet over medium-high heat. Brown short ribs in batches on all sides, about 10 minutes. Remove ribs from pan; drain fat. Add the water and chicken stock. Stir, scraping up the browned bits on the bottom of the pan. Place ribs back in pan and heat liquid to a simmer.

3   Cover and place in the oven. Cook for 2 to 2½ hours or until ribs are very tender. Remove ribs from liquid and cool slightly. Break meat into large chunks, discarding bones, fat, and membrane; set meat aside. Reserve liquid for ragu.

recipe continued on page 102

recipe continued from page 101

4 For the ragu, heat olive oil in a large sauté pan over medium heat. Add garlic and cook and stir until it starts to turn golden brown, about 30 seconds. Add meat and cook for 1 to 2 minutes. (Don't worry if meat sticks to the pan; the liquid will help release it.)

5 Add tomatoes, 1 cup of the reserved braising liquid, cream, oregano, salt, and pepper, stirring to combine. Bring to a simmer, and cook and reduce for 5 minutes.

6 To serve, bring a large pot of salted water to a boil. Add cracked pepper pappardelle and stir to separate noodles. Cook for 45 seconds to 1 minute, stirring to separate ribbons of pasta; drain. When sauce has reduced, add drained pasta to sauce; toss to coat.

7 To serve, use tongs to divide pasta among four shallow bowls. Arrange pieces of beef on top of pasta. Use a rubber scraper to transfer remaining sauce to top of pasta.

8 Garnish each serving with chives and shaved Parmesan.

Egg yolks give homemade black pepper-speckled pappardelle a rich flavor, a chewy texture, and a beautiful yellow hue.

cracked pepper pappardelle

Prep: 30 minutes   **Stand:** 1 hour + 10 minutes   **Makes:** 4 servings

1   cup semolina flour
¼   cup "00" flour*
¼   cup water
2   large egg yolks
5   teaspoons extra virgin olive oil
½   teaspoon kosher salt
½   teaspoon cracked black pepper

1 Combine flours, the water, egg yolks, olive oil, salt, and pepper in a food processor. Pulse until mixture comes together in a ball, adding more water 1 tablespoon at a time if necessary.

2 On a lightly floured surface, gently knead dough until it is smooth and elastic, about 5 to 6 minutes. Wrap dough in plastic wrap and let stand at room temperature for 1 hour.

3 To use a pasta machine, divide dough in quarters. Process dough according to manufacturer's directions to create four thin sheets of pasta. To roll the pasta by hand, on a lightly floured surface roll whole ball of dough with a rolling pin into a sheet, turning occasionally, until you can see your fingers through the bottom. Let dry 10 minutes.

4 Dust the sheet(s) of dough lightly with flour and loosely roll into a flattened cylinder(s). Using a sharp knife, cut off any rough edges. Cut pasta into ¾-inch-wide slices. Unwrap noodles. Toss lightly with flour to keep noodles from sticking. Place on a sheet pan and cover with a clean, damp kitchen towel until ready to use.

*tip This is a very finely textured flour imported from Italy. Look for "00" flour at specialty shops.

cedar plank-roasted halibut with caramelized squash farro

Cooking foods on cedar planks does two things: It infuses the fish, poultry, or meat with a pleasant, smoky flavor and also keeps it moist, as the water in the soaked planks evaporates into the food during cooking.

Prep: 30 minutes   **Roast:** 15 minutes   **Cook:** 25 minutes   **Makes:** 4 servings

1	pound fresh asparagus, trimmed
1	tablespoon extra virgin olive oil
	kosher salt
	ground black pepper
4	cedar grilling planks, soaked in water for 1 to 2 hours
4	tablespoons butter, softened
4	6-ounce halibut fillets, skin removed
2	tablespoons butter toasted farro (see recipe, below)
1	cup heavy whipping cream
1	cup roasted butternut squash (see recipe, page 118)
1	teaspoon smoked paprika
6	cups baby kale
½	cup grated Parmesan cheese

1 Preheat oven to 450°F. Toss asparagus with olive oil; season to taste with salt and black pepper. Arrange in a single layer on a large rimmed baking sheet. Place on rack in lower third of oven. Roast for 15 minutes or until crisp-tender, using tongs to lightly toss twice during roasting.

2 Meanwhile, remove cedar planks from water and shake off excess. Spread 2 tablespoons of the softened butter over the tops of the planks. Sprinkle salt and pepper over the butter. Place halibut fillets on the planks. Spread remaining 2 tablespoons softened butter over fillets. Season lightly with salt and pepper.

3 Roast on rack in upper third of oven for 10 minutes or until done (fish flakes easily with a fork).

4 While asparagus and fish are roasting, melt 2 tablespoons butter in a large sauté pan over medium heat. Add toasted farro and stir until warm, about 1 minute. Add cream, roasted butternut squash, salt and pepper to taste, paprika, and kale. Cook and gently stir for about 1 minute, until kale is just wilted. Add Parmesan and stir to combine, about 30 seconds.

5 To serve, divide squash-farro mixture among four dinner plates, placing in the center of each plate. Top with asparagus. Remove halibut fillets from cedar planks and place across the asparagus.

toasted farro Toast 1 cup uncooked farro in a large skillet over medium-high heat, stirring occasionally, until aromatic and golden brown, about 5 minutes. Transfer toasted farro to a medium saucepan. Add 3 cups water and ½ teaspoon salt. Cover and bring to a boil; reduce heat to low. Simmer and cook until tender, about 20 to 25 minutes. Drain well. Transfer to a bowl; set aside. (This can be done up to 2 days ahead. Store in a tightly sealed container in the refrigerator.)

A sun-dappled patch of micro basil brightens a spot in an organic garden.

greek yogurt panna cotta with fresh pomegranate

Homemade graham crackers are best for the crumble, but if you are short on time, you can certainly use purchased graham crackers.

Prep: 15 minutes   **Cook:** 1 hour   **Chill:** 30 minutes + 4 hours   **Bake:** 10 minutes   **Makes:** 8 servings

pomegranate syrup

4 cups pomegranate juice
2 tablespoons fresh lemon juice
½ cup sugar
1 cup pomegranate seeds

graham crackers

3 cups all-purpose flour
¾ cup sugar
2½ teaspoons baking soda
¼ teaspoon cinnamon
¾ cup old-fashioned oats
1 cup plus 2 tablespoons graham flour
⅔ cup cold butter, cut into chunks
1 tablespoon light corn syrup
2 teaspoons vanilla
½ cup plus 2 tablespoons whole milk
   coarse decorating sugar

yogurt filling

2 8-ounce packages cream cheese, softened
1 cup plain Greek yogurt
½ cup whole milk
3 tablespoons vanilla extract
1 tablespoon lemon juice
½ cup honey

1 For the syrup, combine pomegranate juice, lemon juice, and sugar in a medium saucepan over medium heat. When sugar is completely dissolved, reduce heat to low and let simmer, uncovered, until mixture is reduced by half, about 1 hour. Cool completely. Stir in pomegranate seeds. Store in the refrigerator until ready to use.

2 Preheat oven to 350°F. Line a large rimmed baking sheet with parchment; set aside. For the graham crackers, in a large bowl combine all-purpose flour, sugar, baking soda, cinnamon, oats, and graham flour. Whisk to combine. Using a pastry blender cut butter into the dry ingredients until mixture resembles coarse cornmeal.

3 In a medium bowl combine corn syrup, vanilla, and milk. Add liquid ingredients to dry ingredients. Fold liquid and dry ingredients together with a rubber spatula. Form dough into a flattened ball. Wrap in plastic and chill for 30 minutes.

4 On a lightly floured surface, roll dough into a ¼-inch-thick rectangle. Using a pizza or pastry cutter, cut into 3×3-inch squares. Transfer squares to prepared baking sheet. Sprinkle with coarse sugar, pressing lightly to adhere. Bake for 10 to 12 minutes or until crackers are light golden brown. Let cool on baking sheet 5 minutes. Transfer to a wire rack to cool completely. (You will get 18 crackers; save the extras for another use.)

5 For yogurt filling, beat cream cheese in a large bowl on medium-high until smooth, about 3 minutes, occasionally scraping down the sides of the bowl. Add yogurt, milk, vanilla, lemon juice, and honey. Continue beating until mixture is creamy and smooth. Store in an airtight container in the refrigerator until very cold, about 4 hours.

6 To assemble parfaits, break one graham cracker into small pieces in the bottom of a 4-inch glass Mason jar. Top with ½ cup of the yogurt filling. Drizzle generously with pomegranate syrup. Top with additional cracker crumbs, if desired. Serve immediately.

white chocolate-peppermint hot chocolate

This rich and creamy drink made with white chocolate, whipping cream, whole milk, and vanilla bean is a true holiday treat. Serve with gingersnaps for dipping, if you like.

Start to finish: 10 minutes   **Makes:** 4 servings

2   cups white chocolate chips
2   cups heavy whipping cream
2   cups whole milk
½   of a vanilla bean, split lengthwise
1   teaspoon vanilla extract
     whipped cream, for garnish
¼   cup crushed peppermint candies, for garnish
4   peppermint sticks

1 In a medium saucepan combine chocolate chips and heavy cream. Place over medium heat and stir until chocolate is completely melted. Add milk, vanilla bean, and vanilla extract. Continue to stir until hot and steaming.

2 Divide milk mixture among four mugs. Garnish with whipped cream and crushed peppermint candy. Place a peppermint stick in each mug. Serve immediately.

winter white sangria

Sangria is not a summer-only refresher. This cool-weather sipper is made with Chardonnay and rum and served studded with red grapes and a basil leaf for garnish.

Prep: 10 minutes   **Chill:** 2 hours   **Makes:** 8 to 9 servings

sangria mix
1½ cups St. Germain (elderflower liqueur)
1   cup white rum
1   bottle Chardonnay, chilled
1   cup fresh agave sour (see recipe, below)

to serve
ice
red grapes
large basil leaves

1 In a 2-quart covered pitcher combine elderflower liqueur, rum, Chardonnay, and fresh agave sour. Stir to combine; chill until cold, about 2 to 4 hours.

2 To serve, fill a cocktail shaker half full with ice. Add 4 halved grapes, 1 torn basil leaf, and 6 ounces sangria mix to shaker. Cover and shake vigorously for 15 seconds. Pour into a 12-ounce Tom Collins glass (do not strain). Add more ice, if needed. Garnish with a whole basil leaf and serve immediately.

fresh agave sour In a small jar combine ½ cup agave nectar and ½ cup fresh lime juice. Cover and shake gently to combine. Makes 1 cup.

basic recipes

Restaurant kitchens rely on a collection of foundational recipes – such as sauces and salad dressings – that are often used in multiple dishes on their menus. A few of these recipes can be enjoyed on their own, but most are used as an integral part of another recipe.

neapolitan pizza sauce

Start to Finish: 10 minutes   **Makes:** 3 cups

1   28-ounce can crushed San Marzano tomatoes, drained
3   tablespoons extra virgin olive oil
¼   cup chiffonade-cut fresh basil*
¼   teaspoon chopped fresh thyme leaves

In a medium bowl combine tomatoes, olive oil, basil, and thyme. Stir until thoroughly combined.

*tip Chiffonade means "made of rags" in French. To cut basil in chiffonade, stack the leaves on top of each another, then roll up starting on a long side. Cut the roll into thin slices.

lemon-herb vinaigrette

Start to Finish: 15 minutes   **Makes:** about 1 cup

3   tablespoons fresh lemon juice
3   tablespoons red wine vinegar
1   tablespoon sugar
1   large garlic clove, chopped
1½   teaspoons dried oregano
½   teaspoon kosher salt
½   teaspoon cracked black pepper
¾   cup extra virgin olive oil

In a blender container, combine lemon juice, vinegar, sugar, garlic, oregano, salt, and pepper. With blender running on high, slowly add oil in a very thin stream until vinaigrette is thickened and smooth. Store in a tightly sealed container in the refrigerator for up to 3 days.

tarragon vinaigrette

Start to Finish: 5 minutes   **Makes:** ½ cup

2   tablespoons fresh lemon juice
2   tablespoons minced shallot
1   tablespoon finely chopped tarragon
½   teaspoon kosher salt
½   teaspoon cracked black pepper
½   cup extra virgin olive oil

In a medium bowl combine lemon juice, shallot, tarragon, salt, and pepper. Slowly whisk in olive oil in a thin stream until well blended and slightly thickened. (Or combine all ingredients in a screw-top jar and shake until combined.) Store in a tightly sealed container in the refrigerator for up to 2 days.

crispy roasted fingerling potatoes

Prep: 10 minutes   **Roast:** 25 minutes   **Makes:** 6 to 8 servings

2   pounds small fingerling potatoes, halved lengthwise
3   tablespoons extra virgin olive oil
½   teaspoon kosher salt
½   teaspoon cracked black pepper

Preheat oven to 425°F. In a large bowl toss potatoes with olive oil, salt, and pepper. Transfer potatoes to a large rimmed baking pan, cut sides up, in a single layer. Roast for 25 to 30 minutes, rotating pan halfway through baking time. Continue to roast until potatoes are browned and crisp on the outside and tender when pierced with a fork.

roasted butternut squash

Prep: 20 minutes   **Roast:** 20 minutes   **Makes:** 4 to 6 servings

1   butternut squash
    (2 pounds), peeled,
    seeded, and cut into
    ¾-inch cubes
1   tablespoon extra virgin
    olive oil
½   teaspoon kosher salt
¼   teaspoon cracked black
    pepper

Preheat oven to 450°F. In a large bowl toss squash with olive oil, salt, and pepper. Transfer squash to a large rimmed baking pan in a single layer. Roast for 20 minutes, stirring occasionally, until squash is tender but still firm and lightly browned on the edges.

caramelized onions

Prep: 5 minutes   **Cook:** 15 minutes

1   tablespoon unsalted butter
1   medium yellow onion,
    halved and thinly sliced
    kosher salt
    cracked black pepper

In a medium skillet melt butter over medium heat. Add onion and reduce heat to medium-low. Season with salt and pepper. Cook, stirring occasionally, until onion is golden brown and caramelized, about 15 minutes.

roasted garlic

Prep: 5 minutes   **Roast:** 35 minutes

1   large head garlic
1   tablespoon extra virgin
    olive oil

Preheat oven to 400°F. Cut ¼ inch off of top (narrow end) of a large head of garlic. Remove any loose papery skins. Place garlic head on a piece of aluminum foil. Drizzle with olive oil. Wrap tightly in foil. Roast for 35 to 40 minutes. Unwrap and let cool. Garlic should be golden-brown in color and tender. Use as directed in recipe.

index